PRAYERS
FOR THE
JOURNEY

Fr James FitzPatrick, O.M.I., an Australian Oblate of Mary Immaculate, was ordained in 1959. After postgraduate studies in Rome, Paris and St Louis, USA, he spent thirteen years in teaching and educational administration in Australia. For ten years he was the National Director of the Catholic Enquiry Centre. Elected to the Oblate General Administration in Rome, he also worked on thirty-one causes of canonization. He has been engaged in retreats and parish missions worldwide. He is currently based in Melbourne, Australia.

PRAYERS
FOR THE
JOURNEY

James M. FitzPatrick, O.M.I.

First published in Great Britain in 2008

Society for Promoting Christian Knowledge
36 Causton Street
London SW1P 4ST

Text copyright © James M. FitzPatrick O.M.I. 2007, 2008

Illustrations copyright © Dorothy Woodward R.S.J. 2007, 2008

Original edition published in Australia in 2007 by St Pauls Publications, PO Box 906,
Strathfield, NSW 2135, Australia

Nihil Obstat: The Revd John Flader
Imprimatur: † George Cardinal Pell, Archbishop of Sydney, 19 September 2007

The Nihil Obstat and Imprimatur are a declaration that a book or pamphlet is considered
to be free from doctrinal or moral error. It is not necessarily implied that those who have
granted them agree with the contents, opinions or statements expressed.

SPCK does not necessarily endorse the individual views contained in its publications.

Scripture references are from the New Revised Standard Version copyright © 1989, 1995 by
the Division of Christian Education of the National Council of the Churches of Christ in
the United States of America. Used by permission. All rights reserved.

British Library Cataloguing-in-Publication Data
A catalogue record for this book is available from the British Library

ISBN 978-0-281-06048-1

10 9 8 7 6 5 4 3 2 1

Printed in China

INTRODUCTION

Praying is heart to heart time, soul to soul time, lover to lover time. To pray is to pause in God's presence, speaking, listening, basking in the divine closeness. It can take many forms and should be as individual as the person who is praying. It is simply about you and God, and God and you.

As you enter into prayer some written words can be of help – to catch your attention, to stir your heart and mind, to lead you into the inner reaches of your spirit. Don't just recite prayers or say the words. Use them to enter into a dialogue which rises and moves beyond words. They are but a starting point, an opening of a door. They are seeds that grow into wondrous harvests if you hold them and are held by them.

These "Prayers for the Journey" are original prayers offered simply as little passages to help you focus, to gather up your daily cares and concerns, to invite you to turn to the God who loves you. Use them as springboards, as steps on your journey. Read them for what they suggest, savour them for what they inspire, sit quietly and comfortably with them. Be drawn closer to the One who is your beginning and your end, your creator and Saviour, your greatest good and highest glory. Praying is being with God.

James M. FitzPatrick, O.M.I.

SUGGESTIONS FOR USE

This book of prayers has an original prayer for each day of the year. The fifty-two weeks of the year are grouped under the twelve months. A theme is assigned to each week to serve as a focus for the seven days. Some of the prayers relate more directly to the theme, others are part of a continuing dialogue with God.

Because of changing dates, e.g. Lent, Easter, you may wish to move those sets of weekly prayers around depending on the dates of those feasts for the particular year. However, as in any chat with a friend, don't be too restricted by dates or themes. The conversation flows where the heart moves. These prayers are a means to an end and that end is to draw you closer to the God who is the breath of life for your soul.

Refer to the prayer for the day. Try if possible, to allocate a regular time for it – as you put on your shoes in the morning, with the family at breakfast or dinner, over a cup of morning tea or coffee, on the train to work and return. Read it, maybe a number of times. Let it speak to you to direct your mind, to touch your heart. Sit with it for a few minutes, then go beyond the words to take up your own thoughts leading to your conversation with God. Stay with God. Maybe refer back to the prayer again. Continue to stay with him for a few minutes, for as long as you need. Recall the prayer at times throughout the day, and return to it as you retire for the night. It then will have blessed your day and bring peace to your night.

As you move through the weeks of the year certain themes or prayers may speak to you in a special way. Mark your favourites. Return to them any time, even over and over again, as your daily living moves you or as individual needs arise.

God is always ready to listen.

JANUARY

"...Christ in you, the hope of glory. It is he whom we proclaim...

    so that we may present everyone mature in Christ."

Col. 1: 27, 28

Sunday

Dear Lord, this is the first week of the New Year.

Like a child new-born it has an uncertain future.

Much is under my control, but some beyond.

May it be a year in which I grow to be –

    more loving, more helpful and more forgiving,

    more prayerful, more faithful and more honourable,

    more generous, more steadfast and more sincere,

    more truthful, more just and more Christ-like.

Grant me the strength of your grace to grow the way I should,

avoiding wrong and doing good to all I meet each day.

Lord, may I walk this New Year with you and for you.

    Amen.

Monday

Dear Lord, I have only just begun,

    and I still have a long way to go.

Give me a push to get on with the job. Amen.

TUESDAY

Dear Lord, the year is new and I stand this day before you,
Conscious that, in a very real way, you stand behind me too.
   Amen.

WEDNESDAY

I see you, Lord, as this New Year dawns –
      in the rising of the sun, in the shining of the moon,
      in the falling of the rain, in the pounding of the waves,
      in the blue of the sky, in the turning of the seasons.
And I thank you, Lord, for all these gifts. Amen.

THURSDAY

Thy will, my will.
Lord, help me keep them both the same. Amen.

FRIDAY

Light shines to point the way, light shines to brighten the dark.
Light shines to show the beauty, light shines to warn of danger.
Light shines to cheer the spirit, light shines to enable our steps.
Lord, you are the light that shines.
Be there always for me on my journey. Amen.

SATURDAY

Jesus is Lord.
Enough said. Amen.

WEEK 2 MY LIFE OF FAITH

"Everyone who believes that Jesus is the Christ has been born of
God...this is the victory that conquers the world, our faith."
I JOHN 5:1, 4

SUNDAY

Lord, may I know you with my mind,
may I hold you in my heart,
may I profess you with my lips,
and may every act of mine in faith
be always for your glory. Amen.

MONDAY

Mary received the angel's word – and it came to be when
her child was formed.
May I receive the Word of God – and may it come to life in me.
Amen.

TUESDAY

When springtime blooms and all is bright,
I think of you, Lord, and your wonderful light.
When eagles soar and birds take flight,
I lift my eyes and rejoice in your might. Amen.

WEDNESDAY

I believe out of faith.

Help me to act out of faith. Amen.

THURSDAY

Jesus is before me to lead me.

Jesus is behind me to support me.

Jesus is beside me to walk with me.

Together we can journey far. Amen.

FRIDAY

Jesus is the greatest lover of all time.

May his love in me be fruitful. Amen.

SATURDAY

Lord, you are immense and I'm just a little one.

Thanks for staying with me. Amen.

WEEK 3 PRAISE BE TO GOD

*"Blessing and glory and wisdom and thanksgiving and honour
and power and might be to our God for ever and ever. Amen."*

Rev. 7: 12

Sunday

Whenever I'm touched by the sun's warm ray,

Whenever I wake to another day,

Whenever I feel the cool breeze blow,

Whenever I marvel at stars aglow,

Whenever I smell the rain-soaked earth,

Whenever I see a child at birth,

Whenever I stand with heart upraised –

May you, my God, be always praised. Amen.

Monday

Praise God for the wonders of creation.

Praise God for the gift of our salvation.

Praise God for the good, the great, the best.

Praise God for the joy of promised rest.

Praise God for he is worthy of all praise.

Praise God for now and all the length of days. Amen.

TUESDAY

Praise be to God in all life's days,
For he has loved me in all his ways.
Praise him on high with mighty voice,
And in his love let me rejoice. Amen.

WEDNESDAY

The goodness of God delights me.
The love of God overwhelms me.
The mercy of God restores me.
By all three I am comforted,
through all three I am sustained.
In all three I will glory. Amen.

THURSDAY

The soil beneath my feet, the sky above my head,
both are God's gifts. Thank you, Lord. Amen.

FRIDAY

O Lord, the sights of the world are your shadow,
The sounds of the earth are your echo.
    Your wonders surround me,
    Your presence around me,
Your glory and power daily flow. Amen.

SATURDAY

The sun, the moon, the stars, all tell of you, Lord.
May I, in my own little way, tell of you too. Amen.

WEEK 4 | DEDICATE THE DAY

"Come to me, all you that are weary and are carrying
heavy burdens, and I will give you rest."
MATT. 11: 28

SUNDAY

Dear Lord, you have given me a new day,
and with it comes the promise of
>God to be adored, others to be helped,
>good to be done, gifts to be given,
>love to be expressed, joy to be shared,
>friendships to be enjoyed, lonely to be comforted,
>kindness to be shown, happiness to be passed on,
>forgiveness to be asked for, pardon to be granted,
>hope to be offered, gentleness to be exercised,
>blessings to be imparted, praise to be expressed,
>justice to be upheld, truth to be told,
>thanks to be rendered, life to be lived.

Oh! What a day you and I are going to have together, Lord!
>Amen.

MONDAY

Feet are for walking, mouth is for talking.
Dear Lord, help me not put one into the other. Amen.

TUESDAY

Dear Lord, I am awake as this new day dawns.

Help me to be awake to those who love me, to those who
    need me.

But most of all, help me this day to be awake to you. Amen.

WEDNESDAY

If I can live today without hurting others,
    it will be a day well spent, Lord.

If I can live today uplifting others,
    it will be a day well spent, Lord.

If I can live today showing you to others,
    it will be a day well spent, Lord. Amen.

THURSDAY

Be with me, Lord, at first light dawning.

Be with me, Lord, under noon-time sun.

Be with me, Lord, as evening stills the day.

Be with me, Lord, when night wraps all in dark.

May all my times – morn, noon, eve and night –

be always lived with you, Lord, for you are
    creator of them all. Amen.

FRIDAY

Day comes, day goes.
God loves, life flows.
Thank you, Lord. Amen.

SATURDAY

Day begun, day ended.
How much for you, Lord? Amen.

WEEK 5 THANKS BE TO GOD (I)

"As you… have received Christ Jesus the Lord, continue to
live your lives in him…abounding in thanksgiving."
Col. 2: 6, 7

SUNDAY

I thank you, Lord,
>for all that was,
>for all that is,
>for all that will be.
All times are in your hands. Amen.

MONDAY

God, you give me so much and so freely –
>my life, my world, my family.
But one gift above all I thank you for –
>your gift to me of redemption. Amen.

TUESDAY

Christ in the manger –
>the world is awakened.
Christ on the cross –
>the world is redeemed.
Christ in his heaven –
>the world is saved.
Thank you, Lord, thank you. Amen.

Wednesday

Lord, I thank you for the gift of friends,

    for the cheerful smile,

    for the joy of company,

    for the supporting hands,

    for the warmth of trust,

    for the accepting love,

    for the words of truth.

And may I be likewise friend to them. Amen.

Thursday

Who was born so that he should die?

Who was imprisoned to set others free?

Who was wounded so that we should be healed?

Who was scourged so that others should be comforted?

Who was put to death so that all should come to life?

Who came down from above so that he should rise up again?

Only God, my loving God, would do this.

And he did it for me! Amen.

Friday

Created, redeemed and loved –

For all these I thank you, Lord. Amen.

SATURDAY

Lord, I turn to you in faith, in hope, in love.

I have failed you by my deeds and by my neglect.

Thank you for standing ready to welcome me back yet again

to believe in you, to trust in you, to love you. Amen.

FEBRUARY

WEEK 6 TRUST IN MY GOD

"…I put my trust in you. In God whose word I
praise, in God I trust; I am not afraid."

Ps. 56: 3, 4

SUNDAY

I have trust in you, Lord, for all that you have made,
for all that you have given, for all that you have promised.
But most of all, I have trust in you for all that you are.
Amen.

MONDAY

I place my trust in you, Lord,
when the sun is darkened,
when the moon is hidden,
when the stars don't shine,
when the birds don't sing,
when the leaves turn brown,
when the little ones die.
For, in face of these,
I know that life is in your hands,
and that all your loving care
is there alive – and for me. Amen.

TUESDAY

I believe in you God, the Father Almighty.

Help me to know that you believe in me too. Amen.

WEDNESDAY

I looked, and you were there.

I called, and you answered.

I asked, and you acted.

Lord, I am most blessed. Amen.

THURSDAY

God, you put me on this earth for a purpose.

Not my purpose, but yours.

In you I trust. Amen.

FRIDAY

Home is where heart is.

My heart's with you, Lord. Amen.

SATURDAY

God is loving, can I ever be alone?

God is merciful, can I ever be afraid?

No, never. Amen.

WEEK 7 COURAGE IN LIFE

"I can do all things through him who strengthens me."

PHIL. 4: 13

SUNDAY

Courage to be. Courage to do.
Courage to love. Courage to hope.
Grant me these, O Lord. Amen.

MONDAY

Whatever I do and reach for,
Whatever I have and plan for,
Whatever I think and long for,
I give them freely to you, my Lord,
For then I know that all will be well
in the end. Amen.

TUESDAY

Lord, keep me strong in my belief in you.

Lord, keep me strong in my hope in you.

Lord, keep me strong in my love for you. Amen.

WEDNESDAY

Lord, I face a big world and I am just an ordinary person.

But I have received your grace and that makes me strong.

Help me be courageous in speaking out for you. Amen.

THURSDAY

Christ our Lord, you calmed the sea and put the winds to rest.

Touch now the troubles in me and bring me to a great and
lasting calm. Amen.

FRIDAY

Moses shed his shoes to stand in a holy place –
the place made holy by the presence of his God.

Give me courage to shed whatever mars my soul, my holy place –
the place made holy by the presence of my God. Amen.

SATURDAY

Lord, with love you carried your cross and rose to life.

Give me courage to carry mine, so that I may also rise.
Amen.

WEEK 8 MY DAILY LIFE

"...he who is Lord of heaven and earth...in him
we live and move and have our being."

ACTS 17: 24, 28

SUNDAY

Jesus, you opened the eyes of the blind and the ears of the
deaf. You loosened the tongues of the dumb and gave
strength to the limbs of the lame. Open my eyes to
see you and my ears to hear your message. Loosen my
tongue to praise you and my limbs to be your hands and
feet in the world around me. I ask this in your name.
Amen.

MONDAY

God, our Father, in all things and in all ways,
You are holy.
I ask your grace that in all things and in all ways,
I too may be holy.
Through Christ our Lord. Amen.

TUESDAY

I want this day to be yours, Lord.

Keep me on track to do what's right.

So when the day is past and gone,

I may sleep in peace in a restful night. Amen.

WEDNESDAY

Morning has broken …

Lord, help me keep the rest of my day together. Amen.

THURSDAY

Jesus, you are my way –

    May I never wander from you.

Jesus, you are my truth –

    May I never deny you.

Jesus, you are my life –

    May I never lose you. Amen.

Friday

Lord, help me find myself in the promise of your words,
in the call of the needy, in the love of others.
But above all, help me find myself in you,
the first and last, the foundation and summit, the beginning
and end. Amen.

Saturday

Lord, I've been pretty good today.
Help me be better tomorrow. Amen.

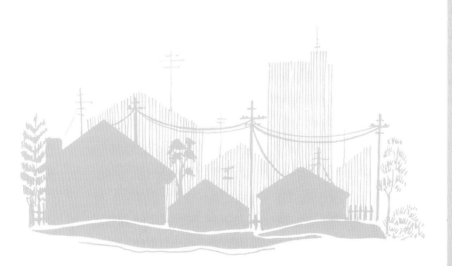

WEEK 9 THE SEASON OF LENT

"Have mercy on me O God, according to your
steadfast love…Create in me a clean heart, O
God, and put a new and right spirit in me."

Ps. 51: 1, 10

SUNDAY

Your whole life, Lord, was a preparation for your passion,
death and resurrection.

I now have these forty days of Lent to prepare myself to
stand with you.

Help me to live these mysteries with a sense of fervour,
gratitude and awe. Amen.

MONDAY

He who is most powerful became a man of weakness.

He who is most loving became an object of hate.

He who is most blessed became as one cursed.

He who is most healing became a mass of wounds.

He who is most exalted became as one despised.

He who is most glorious became a thing of shame.

He is my God, my Saviour and Redeemer, Jesus Christ.

In that saving and redeeming he gave his all. Amen.

TUESDAY

Lord, I have sinned,

    by thought and by deed,

    by word and by silence,

    by act and by omission.

As often as I have sinned

you have stood ready to forgive.

O gracious Lord, I thank you. Amen.

WEDNESDAY

Lord, I am tempted to turn from you.
Be now my strength that I may not sin.
Draw me back to stand by you,
And let not evil enter in. Amen.

THURSDAY

Lord, I have sinned.
Love me still. Amen.

FRIDAY

Lord, in your life you changed
    sickness to health,
    sorrow to joy,
    death to life.
Change now in me those things
which only your love can heal. Amen.

SATURDAY

I thank you, Lord, for your forgiveness,

    when I neglected you,

    when I strayed from you,

    when I offended you,

    when I thought only of myself.

And now, Lord, it's good to be back with you again. Amen.

MARCH

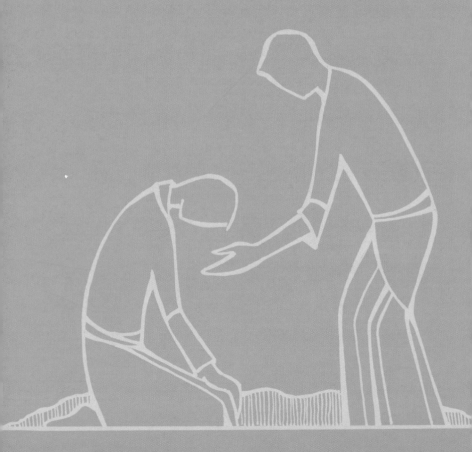

WEEK 10 I AM FORGIVEN

"The Lord is merciful and gracious, slow to anger and abounding
in steadfast love...He does not deal with us according
to our sins, nor repay us according to our iniquities."

Ps. 103: 8, 10

SUNDAY

Jesus died for me.
Jesus *died* for me.
Jesus died *for me*. Amen.

MONDAY

Loving and saving Jesus, you came to me.
Loved and saved, Jesus, I go to you. Amen.

TUESDAY

Dear Lord, when others turn from me,
   help me to remember that you love me.
Even when I turn from you,
   help me to remember that you love me. Amen.

WEDNESDAY

Sometimes I am tempted to put other things
 in place of you, Lord.
    to see them as more desirable,
    to enjoy the fleeting moment.
Lord, help me keep my head straight,
And my heart in the right place. Amen.

THURSDAY

Lord, I am sorry for the pain and hurt that I have caused others.
But most of all, I am sorry that I have offended you. Amen.

FRIDAY

Tears are words that are not spoken.
May my tears tell of my sorrow for what I have done,
and may I thank you for your forgiveness. Amen.

SATURDAY

God is love….Wow! Amen.

WEEK 11 I FORGIVE

"Do not judge, and you will not be judged; do not condemn, and
you will not be condemned. Forgive, and you will be forgiven."

Luke 6: 37

SUNDAY

Lord, you gave us a new command –
that we should love one another.
May I be at one with you in forgiving,
For in this my love is truly tested. Amen.

MONDAY

To love as I am loved,
to bless as I am blessed,
to forgive as I am forgiven,
for these I strive, Lord. Amen.

TUESDAY

Lord, help me to forgive those who hurt me,
lest I be tempted to hurt them back. Amen.

WEDNESDAY

To love is to give, to love is to forgive.
May my hands and my heart be always open. Amen.

Thursday

I love others because God loves them, and loves me.
I bless others because God blesses them, and blesses me.
I forgive others because God forgives them, and forgives me.
Keep me constant, Lord, as I walk through life. Amen.

Friday

Lord, I'm often too ready to fire back an insult.
Lord, keep me patient and forgiving. Amen.

Saturday

Lord, help me to be more ready to forgive –
    to forgive neglect, insults, ingratitude.
You suffered all of these, Lord, on this earth
    and you forgave those who did these wrongs.
Help me also to be forgiving as you are. Amen.

WEEK 12 MY PRAYER

"Do not lag in zeal, be ardent in spirit, serve the Lord. Rejoice in hope, be patient in suffering, persevere in prayer."

ROM. 12: 11-12

SUNDAY

Lord, help me to slow down and make some space,
    space for friends, space for silence,
    space for helping, space for quiet,
    space for caring, space for calm.
And more than anything else, help me make a lot more
    space for you. Amen.

MONDAY

The blue of the sky,
the green of the trees,
the red of the roses,
the gold of the wheat,
all help paint your picture, Lord. Amen.

TUESDAY

I am always happy to talk about God,
But much happier when I talk to God. Amen.

WEDNESDAY

"Glory to God in the highest" signalled the coming of
    Christ to our world.
May I keep the glory of God at the heart of my prayer,
And show to our world the glory that truly is Christ. Amen.

THURSDAY

Jesus, I learnt of you when just a child, and I loved you.
As I grew I prayed to you, I sometimes strayed from you,
    I turned to you in need.
Lord Jesus, keep us together on life's journey, together in
    love. Amen.

FRIDAY

Lord, make me wise as you are wise,
not just in the things of this world,
but in the wisdom of the heart. Amen.

SATURDAY

Hi, Lord, it's me again.

Great to be with you.

Let's keep in touch. Amen.

WEEK 13 THE GIFT OF REDEMPTION

"…we were reconciled to God through the death
of his Son, much more surely, having been
reconciled, will we be saved by his life."

R OM. 5: 10

S UNDAY

Jesus knelt to wash the feet of his apostles.
He who is King and Saviour knelt.
May I so serve as he did them,
and follow the example of my Redeemer. Amen.

M ONDAY

Lord Jesus, you died for me to save me.
May I live for you to serve you. Amen.

T UESDAY

I am created, I am loved.
I am graced, I am redeemed.
For all these I thank you, Lord. Amen.

W EDNESDAY

Lord, you have given me so many gifts.
For these I am grateful indeed.
Yes for the gifts, but more so for the Giver. Amen.

THURSDAY

We have already gained our reconciliation,
  won for us through the death of God's Son.
Dear Lord, may the truth of this
  envelop me, confirm me, strengthen me,
  overwhelm me, uplift me, grace me.
And may I reach out exultantly for the glory of your gift.
  Amen.

FRIDAY

May I live with you, Lord,
love with you, Lord,
and always walk beside you, Lord.
  Amen.

SATURDAY

Jesus sat at table with his apostles
and he fed them with the bread of life,
the life that he was to give to redeem us all.
May I always have a place there with him
and be blessed to eat of that same bread,
the bread that will nourish me unto eternity. Amen.

APRIL

"…through him God was pleased to reconcile to himself
all things, whether on earth or in heaven, by
making peace through the blood of his cross."

Col. 1: 20

Sunday

There was a Cross in the mind of God
    before the coming of Christ,
  for God foresaw that humankind would need to be saved.
There was a Cross on the crest of the hill of Calvary,
  for only a God-made-man could pay the price
    of redemption.
There needs be a Cross vibrant in the depths of my heart,
  calling me to thank my God for the gift of salvation.
  Amen.

Monday

The scourge, the thorns, the Cross –
All for me. Thank you, Lord. Amen.

Tuesday

The Cross of Jesus is my tree of life.
May he who hung upon it be always alive to me. Amen.

Wednesday

Dear Lord, you died on the Cross for sinners.
Dear Lord, you died on the Cross for me. Amen.

Thursday

Dear Jesus, when I am exhausted, bothered,
    stressed and tired, I sit in the shade of a tree.
Dear Jesus, when I am confused, repentant,
    lonely and sad, may I sit in the shade of the Cross.
    Amen.

Friday

When I leave this world, I ask for only one sign
    in my passing –
the sign of the Cross, the Cross of eternal life. Amen.

Saturday

"Stay awake and watch lest you enter into temptation,"
Jesus said to his apostles in the garden of Gethsemane.
Lord, help me be awake to the things that could separate us,
lest I be not mindful of your sacrifice on the Cross. Amen.

WEEK 15 HOLY WEEK

"Let the same mind be in you that was in Christ Jesus...
he humbled himself and became obedient to the
point of death – even death on a cross."

Phil. 2: 5, 8

Sunday

Good Friday tells me that I have a past,

a past needing to be redeemed by a crucified Saviour.

Holy Saturday tells me that I have a present,

a present in waiting to be fulfilled by a loving Saviour.

Easter Sunday tells me that I have a future,

a future won and opened for me by a risen Saviour.

By these holy days I am spared, sustained and saved.

Thank you, Jesus, for the wonders of these days. Amen.

Monday

My Jesus, I look at you upon the Cross.

I see the wounds, the thorns, the scourges.

I seem to hear the shouts, the cries,

I feel the pain, the hate that surges.

TUESDAY

It was for me you chose to die,
For me you gave your life away.
So now I kneel in humble thanks,
And bless each moment of that holy day.

WEDNESDAY

Dear Jesus, help me come to know
The depth of sacrifice you made.
For by the death you died for me,
You for my sins redemption paid. Amen.

THURSDAY

Kings and queens wear crowns of gold.
Yours was of thorns.
Thank you, Lord. Amen.

FRIDAY

Christ lay in the tomb. The world stood still,
about to face the staggering fact
that he would rise to life once more.
    Never before, never again.
Lord, help me grasp this amazing truth
that death in you meant rising to life.
Your majesty overshadows this world of ours.
    Always before, always again. Amen.

SATURDAY

Easter day is about to dawn,
And overtake the night,
When Christ, my Saviour, lives again,
In glory, splendour, light. Amen.

WEEK 16 EASTER

"Blessed be the God and Father of our Lord Jesus Christ! By his great mercy he has given us a new birth into a living hope through the resurrection of Jesus Christ from the dead."

1 PET. 1: 3

SUNDAY

Darkness to light,
sorrow to joy,
sin to salvation.
Resurrection assured. Amen.

MONDAY

Christ died, Christ rose.
I die, I rise.
My thanks to him. Amen.

TUESDAY

Risen Lord, guide me today.
Risen Lord, show me the way.
Risen Lord, keep me true.
Risen Lord, lead me to you. Amen.

WEDNESDAY

They slept that night in the garden of olives
– but Christ rose again.
They ran away and left him all alone
– but Christ rose again.
They called for his death and Pilate gave in
– but Christ rose again.
They scourged him till the blood flowed down
– but Christ rose again.
They pierced his brow with a crown of thorns
– but Christ rose again.
They nailed him to the wood of the cross
– but Christ rose again.
They jeered and laughed and taunted him
– but Christ rose again.
They opened his side with a soldier's lance
– but Christ rose again.
They laid him in a rock-hewn borrowed tomb
– but Christ rose again.
New world, new life, new grace
– and all because Christ rose again.

THURSDAY

Jesus rose on Easter morn.
Have you seen him?

FRIDAY

I see Christ dying, I see Christ rising.
May I see him likewise in those around me. Amen.

SATURDAY

Christ suffered. Christ died.
Christ rose. Christ reigns. Amen.

WEEK 17 THE DAY WITH GOD

*"Those who love me will keep my word, and my
Father will love them, and we will come to
them and make our home with them."*

JOHN 14: 23

SUNDAY

Lord, grant me the grace to see the wonder of you.

Grant me the heart to see the wonder of others.

Grant me the wisdom to see the wonder of me.

Lord, help me to hold sacred the wonder of us all. Amen.

MONDAY

Be with me, Lord, when all goes well.

Be with me, Lord, when the going's tough.

But most of all, be with me, Lord,

when all goes flop! Amen.

TUESDAY

Lord, give me light when all looms dark.

Lord, give me heart when life seems stark.

Lord, give me love when I feel alone.

Lord, give me hope and bring me home. Amen.

WEDNESDAY

I have faith in you, faith in me, faith in us.
Lord, increase my faith. Amen.

THURSDAY

Lord, you walked the years of your life
    to comfort, to heal, to bless.
May I walk the paths of my life
    to bring comfort, healing and blessing. Amen.

FRIDAY

I thank you, Lord, for what you've done with me so far.
Let's work together for even better times ahead. Amen.

SATURDAY

Lord, I'm living my day.
Some of it great, some not too good.
Thanks for the one, sorry for the other. Amen.

MAY

WEEK 18 WITH HIM

"My soul magnifies the Lord….from now on all generations
will call me blessed, for the Mighty One has done
great things for me, and holy is his name."

LUKE 1: 46, 48, 49

SUNDAY

Birds fly – because God made them so to do,
Fish swim – because God made them so to do,
Lambs frolic – because God made them so to do,
Horses gallop – because God made them so to do,
Kangaroos hop – because God made them so to do,
God made me to love. Amen.

MONDAY

Thank you, Lord,
- for the light that illumines the dark,
- for the smiles that dry the tears,
- for the hands that uplift the fallen,
- for the joy that brightens the sorrow,
- for the love that banishes hate. Amen.

Tuesday

Lord, I live by you, I live in you,
I live through you, I live with you,
But, most of all, I live for you.
Keep me with you always. Amen.

Wednesday

Dear Lord, you came into our world to become one like us.
By your coming may we become one like you. Amen.

Thursday

I do not know what tomorrow may bring.
But I have confidence that you will be there with me.
That's all I need to know. Amen.

Friday

Lord, you are calling me to live with your life in this world.
Please, Lord, call a little louder, and more insistently. Amen.

Saturday

My prayers often raise questions.
God's answers are better. Amen.

WEEK 19 WITH THE SAINTS

"…let your light shine before others, so that they may see your good works and give glory to your Father in heaven."

MATT. 5: 16

SUNDAY

I see the saints in stained-glass window panes.
They let the light of God shine through.
In colours varied, bright and clear,
More vibrant, more than artist ever drew.

MONDAY

The saints are prisms of God's light
In shades of red, green, blue and gold.
Each one a grace-filled child of him,
To shine his light and us enfold.

TUESDAY

Keep me transparent, Lord,
    in all I do,
Lest by my sin I block your light,
For I need shine for all to see,
To show the good, the true, the right.

WEDNESDAY

The saints are those who let the light,
The light of God, shine through.
May I be blessed to be like them,
Let shine the light, the light of you. Amen.

THURSDAY

God is calling me to be holy.
Am I listening? Amen.

FRIDAY

Holiness is not just not sinning.
Holiness is loving, and loving, and loving. Amen.

SATURDAY

None of us are born saints.
That comes with time,
with many mistakes and graces along the way.

For every saint has a past.
But by your bounty, Lord,
And with the passing of the years
I pray that I may be ripe for heaven.

For every sinner has a future. Amen.

WEEK 20 I PRAY FOR OTHERS (I)

"I thank my God every time I remember you, constantly praying
with joy in every one of my prayers for all of you…"

PHIL. 1: 3,4

SUNDAY

Grant Lord, that I see you in the beauty of creation,

    hear you in the sounds of the forest,

    touch you in the texture of the earth,

    smell you in the fragrance of the flowers,

    taste you in the fruit of the fields.

But grant also Lord, that I may

    see you in the faces of the helpless,

    hear you in the cries of the weak,

    touch you in the hands of the dispossessed,

    smell you in the sourness of poverty,

    taste you in the bitterness of defeat.

Lord, help me to sense you in all of these,

and may I also be present there for you. Amen.

MONDAY

Lord, I am happy today

Help me make others happy too. Amen.

TUESDAY

My hands are for lifting up, not pushing down.

My hands are for supporting, not letting fall.

My hands are for applauding, not striking.

Lord, help me to hold gently all those around me. Amen.

WEDNESDAY

I don't know who's hurting today, Lord.

Whoever they may be, I pray for them. Amen.

THURSDAY

Dear Lord, I seem to be mightily concerned with me.

Help me to reach beyond my little world of self.

Help me to live for others, especially in their need.

But every day, help me reach up to you. Amen.

FRIDAY

Dear Lord, you love me with a love that only you can give.

Help me to love others fully, kindly, and just for their sake.
Amen.

SATURDAY

Lord, teach me to open myself to love, to love all those

- to whom I owe the love of gratitude,
- to whom I owe the love of fidelity,
- to whom I owe the love of responsibility,
- to whom I owe the love of thanksgiving,
- to whom I owe the love of care,
- to whom I owe the love of pardon,
- to whom I owe the love of forgiveness,

for in loving these I become a little more like you. Amen.

WEEK 21 FOR PEACE (I)

"Jesus Christ...came and proclaimed peace to you who
were far off and peace to those who were near..."

EPH. 2: 17

SUNDAY

Peace comes from justice, from equity and right.

Peace comes from gentleness, from calmness and respect.

Peace comes from selflessness, from acceptance and love.

Peace comes from loyalty, from fairness and truth.

From these peace is born and in them bears its fruit.

Dear Lord, may I be always a source of peace. Amen.

MONDAY

Lord, speak to me, so that I can learn wisdom from you.

Lord, speak in me, so that my spirit may be filled with you.

Lord, speak with me, so that I may never be alone or lost.

Lord, speak by me, so that I may pass on a love of you.

Lord, speak through me, so that I may be a light to others.

Lord, speak for me, so that I may bring your peace to all.

   Amen.

TUESDAY

Lord, I have but one life.

May it find its peace in you. Amen.

WEDNESDAY

Faith lasts until all come home to God.

Hope lasts until his words are fulfilled.

Love lasts forever unto eternal life.

In these I find true peace. Amen.

THURSDAY

"Peace be with you," said the risen Christ.

I pray for peace in my family, in my workplace, in my
country.

But in the foremost place, I pray for true peace in the
depths of my mind,

in the core of my heart, and in my inmost spirit. Amen.

FRIDAY

Dear Lord, love me and help me love others.

Dear Lord, care for me and help me care for others.

Dear Lord, give me peace and help me bring peace to
others. Amen.

SATURDAY

I pray you, Lord, for lasting peace in our divided world.
When race, class, colour, history, religion divide
and lead to warfare,

come into the hearts and minds of those at enmity,

to help them accept that we are all children of the one
God,

and that we are all destined to be one with him. Amen.

WEEK 22 THE HOLY SPIRIT

"...you were marked with the seal of the promised Holy Spirit;
this is the pledge of our inheritance towards redemption
as God's own people, to the praise of his glory."

Eph. 1: 13-14

SUNDAY

Like a strong rushing wind the Spirit came,
To enlighten the minds of all,
To stir up their wills, to stiffen their backs,
To help them answer Christ's call.

Frightened and timid they gathered in fear,
When their Christ was laid in the grave.
But then with the Spirit they rose up again,
To tell of the God who would save.

MONDAY

Come likewise to me, for I need you too
As I live in this world of mine,
To follow the truth, to walk on the way,
To strive for the life divine.

TUESDAY

Inflame me, enlighten, disturb me,
And fill me with holy desire.
Uplift me, possess me and move me to act
With the zeal of your heavenly fire.

WEDNESDAY

Holy Spirit, lead me to where I need go,
Show me the path to be trod,
For when you are with me I never will fear,
For you lead on the pathway to God.

THURSDAY

Oh, give me your power, your strength and your pulse
Today and for days evermore.
With will and resolve I'll hasten my steps
On the way to the God I adore. Amen.

Friday

O Holy Spirit, come to give me your gifts:

- – wisdom, that I may be truly enlightened,
- – understanding, that I may grasp what is essential,
- – knowledge, that I may see God's hand in all,
- – counsel, that I may judge aright in all matters,
- – fortitude, that I may stand strong in perseverance,
- – piety, that I may acknowledge and respect others,
- – fear of the Lord, that I may reverence my God with joy.

Grant me these gifts in abundance,

So that I may abide with you. Amen.

SATURDAY

Holy Spirit, you descended on the Apostles,
to confirm their faith, to strengthen their will,
   to steel their resolve.
Come down on me too with your power,
when I find my belief challenged, when I lose heart,
   when I lack direction.
Enlighten my mind, strengthen my will,
   show clear my path. Amen.

JUNE

WEEK 23 THE BLESSED TRINITY

"Go therefore and make disciples of all nations, baptizing them in the name of the Father and of the Son and of the Holy Spirit."
MATT. 28: 19

SUNDAY

God the Father created me.
God the Son redeemed me.
God the Holy Spirit watches over me.
I am really special.
Thanks to all three. Amen.

MONDAY

The presence of the Father grounds my faith.
The Cross of the Son assures my hope.
The breath of the Spirit enables my love.
With these three and by these three, I journey safe and
    sure. Amen.

TUESDAY

Father, Son, and Spirit, these three, the ever-lasting Trinity.
Before all began, in the years of our time and reaching to
    infinity. Amen.

Wednesday

My world is created by the Father.
My world is redeemed by the Son.
My world is graced by the Spirit.
May I respect it as their gift to me. Amen.

Thursday

Praise God the Father, God the Son, and God the Holy Spirit.
    Praise the Father for his creating and omnipotence,
        for his majesty and glory.
    Praise the Son for his coming and his promises,
        for his death and resurrection.
    Praise the Spirit for his inspiring and confirming,
        for his guiding and blessing.
In all ways and at all times, praise them. Amen.

Friday

Jesus, may I follow you in worshipping your Father.
Jesus, may I follow you in living by your Word.
Jesus, may I follow you by sharing in the Spirit.
Jesus, may I follow you and never ever stray. Amen.

Saturday

Glory be to the Father and to the Son and to the Holy Spirit.
From them all glory comes, to them all glory is forever due.
    Amen.

WEEK 24 GOD'S BLESSINGS

"Ask, and it will be given to you; search, and you will
find; knock, and the door will be opened for you."

LUKE 11: 9

SUNDAY

Bless me in my coming and my going,
Bless me in my rising and in my repose.
Bless me, bless me, Lord.

MONDAY

Bless me in my hurrying and in my stillness,
Bless me in my giving and my receiving.
Bless me, bless me, Lord.

TUESDAY

Bless me in my laughing and my weeping,
Bless me in my strength and my weakness.
Bless me, bless me, Lord.

WEDNESDAY

Bless me in my speaking and my silence,
Bless me in my hoping and remembering.
    Bless me, bless me, Lord.

THURSDAY

Bless me in my being and my doing,
Bless me in my past and in my future.
    Bless me, bless me, Lord. Amen.

FRIDAY

I am blessed in all that I am.
I am blessed in all that I have been given.
I am blessed because you love me, Lord. Amen.

SATURDAY

Bless our bishops – that they be holy and wise.

Bless our priests – that they lead us to God.

Bless our religious – that their lives be in service to others.

Bless our families – that love and care flourish in them.

Bless all men and women – that their lives will be lived in God.

And, dear Lord, bless me – that your grace in me be ever fruitful. Amen.

WEEK 25 THANKS BE TO GOD (II)

"…whatever you do, in word or deed, do everything in the name of the Lord Jesus, giving thanks to God the Father through him."

COL. 3: 17

SUNDAY

Lord, I thank you for so many gifts,
    for you, for others, for me.
May I always use these gifts wisely,
    for you, for others, for me. Amen.

MONDAY

Thanks be to God for the morning light,
for the midday sun, for the evening glow.
May I use them well, and all for you. Amen.

TUESDAY

Love me, Lord, then I am loved above all.
Bless me, Lord, then I am blessed above all.
For these I thank you, Lord, with all my heart. Amen.

WEDNESDAY

Time is on the move.
Lord, help me not to be left behind.
Thanks. Amen.

THURSDAY

The truth of God sets me free.
The love of God keeps me safe.
The hand of God guides me well.
My thanks. Amen.

FRIDAY

I can walk and talk and hear and see and taste and touch.
I can think and feel and smile and cry and savour the
    perfume of the flowers.
For these and all the other things I thank you, Lord,
And pray that I be conscious of you each and every day.
    Amen.

SATURDAY

For the gift of life and salvation, I thank you, Lord.
For the gift of family and friends, I thank you, Lord.
For the gift of being your child, I thank you, Lord.
For all that I am and all that I will be, I thank you, Lord.
    Amen.

WEEK 26 FOR THE SICK

"I consider that the sufferings of this present time are not worth comparing with the glory about to be revealed to us."

ROM. 8: 18

SUNDAY

I pray for the seriously ill who suffer, and for those for
   whom there may be little hope.
Let me be conscious of them, unknown to me though they be,
for I am one with them in our human condition.
> When I am too concerned with me, let my prayer turn
>   to them.
> When I feel tired, let my prayer earn them some rest.
> When I have aches and pains, may my prayer offer them
>   relief.
> When I feel weak, may my prayer give them strength.
> When I am depressed, may my prayer raise up their
>   spirits.
> When I lose hope, may my prayer brighten their day.
Uplift them, Lord, by your kindly presence,
For in their helplessness you alone can sustain them. Amen.

MONDAY

At this very moment, Lord, there are innocent people
    suffering,
little ones neglected, old folks lonely,
people falling sick, families torn apart.
I cannot comfort them all, but let me pray for them now –
    one by one. Amen.

TUESDAY

Lord, I've got my aches and pains – but others are so much
    worse off.
Relieve them, comfort them and make them well.
Give them health of heart and mind and body. Amen.

WEDNESDAY

I pray, Lord, today for those who suffer from mental or
    emotional illness or instability.
May their afflictions, sometimes unseen, be healed or
    contained.
And may they live a life of peace, purpose and happiness.
    Amen.

THURSDAY

Dear Lord, my friend ………..… is dying.

Be with him/her at this most precious time,
  when present life is changing to life anew.

Take my prayers, my love, my caring,
  and place them gently around him/her.

May his/her passing to you be not fraught with fear and
  fright.

May it be made peaceful by your soothing presence.

Lead him/her safely home with you.

Grant him/her eternal rest in the joy of your heavenly
  kingdom. Amen.

FRIDAY

Jesus, you gave consolation and cure to the sick. I thank you
  for your mercy, and ask you to give healing to those who
  are ill. Amen.

SATURDAY

Lord Jesus Christ,

> when you walked this earth you reached out in love to
>
> heal the sick and restore their lives again.
>
> In your mercy look today upon our sick,
>
> give them comfort, and,
>
> if it be your will, grant them healing.
>
> Amen.

JULY

"I am the vine, you are the branches. Those who abide

in me and I in them bear much fruit, because

apart from me you can do nothing."

JOHN 15: 5

SUNDAY

The world around is crowded, busy, loud.

The presence of God is calm, placid, quiet.

Help me to rejoice in you, Lord. Amen.

MONDAY

Dear Lord, I need to rise above myself to look at my life.

Lift me up to you and enlighten me

to learn from where I've been,

to appreciate where I am,

to judge where I ought to go.

Grant this through your kindly help,

For I cannot see it all by myself from down here. Amen.

TUESDAY

"In the beginning was the Word."

Keep speaking, Lord, I'm listening. Amen.

Wednesday

I have asked God for many things,
for health and wealth, for peace and prosperity, for freedom
    and forgiveness.
Yes. Lord, please grant me these, I pray,
but above all else, grant me your greatest gift of all – give
    me yourself. Amen.

Thursday

Jesus, you are with me day by day.
Enfold me in your great and caring love.
You shielded me from evils which around me lay,
unite me with you now with power from above. Amen.

Friday

Lord, keep me whole,
    whole in my life and my living,
    whole in my faith and my loving,
    whole in my joy and my praising.
Yes, Lord, keep me whole, lest I drift away. Amen.

Saturday

With God as my father, Jesus as my brother,
I rest secure in the love of my family. Amen.

"...since we are justified by faith, we have peace with
God through our Lord Jesus Christ...and we boast
in our hope of sharing the glory of God."

ROM. 5: 1-2

SUNDAY

Lord, you came into this world to heal and to give us promises,
and I know that you are faithful in all things.
The promise of the future is the hope of today.
May my future be made bright by the sure hope you give
me today. Amen.

MONDAY

Hope springs eternal in the human breast.
Keep mine bubbling strong, Lord. Amen.

TUESDAY

So often, Lord, I feel let down in many ways.
You are the only final hope I have.
Be there to raise me up, to bring me joy and peace. Amen.

WEDNESDAY

My faith in you, Lord, gives me hope,
and it finds its fulfilment in love. Amen.

THURSDAY

Lord, lots of things don't turn out the way I want them to.
But, dear Lord, I hope that they turn out the way you want
them to. Amen.

FRIDAY

In times of my gladness, my dearest hopes are fulfilled.
In times of my distress, only my hope enables me to carry on.
Dear Lord, may my hope be alive, be real and be founded
only on you. Amen.

SATURDAY

Lord, I'm pretty confused right now.
Sort me out. Amen.

"Blessed be the God and Father of our Lord Jesus Christ, who

has blessed us in Christ with every spiritual blessing..."

EPH. 1: 3

SUNDAY

Lord, it is a simple thing, the pouring of water. But it changed me in depth for ever. I was promised to Christ, accepted by Christ, joined to Christ. From that moment on we walked together through life towards eternity. I am no longer my own person. I am his. I am one with him. Oh, Lord, I thank you from the bottom of my heart. Amen.

MONDAY

At times living my faith gets difficult – temptations, disappointments, failings, distractions. All these draw me away from you, my God. But through his gifts the Spirit strengthens me and gives me the will and the power to soldier on. Holy Spirit, grant me the grace to proclaim the glories of my God and to rest always by his side. Amen.

TUESDAY

Lord Jesus Christ, you came into this world to give us the gift of salvation, the gift of everlasting life. As you were preparing to return to your Father you gave us your final gift – your Body and Blood as our food and drink for eternal life. I bow down in thanksgiving. With you, and you alone, can my eternity be assured. Amen.

WEDNESDAY

Lord, there are times when I do not live by the grace you offer me, and I sin by neglecting you, by choosing others, by putting myself first. I come to you now, conscious of my darkness, but assured of your light. Heal me, cleanse, me, bless me. Renew in me the glory of your presence and make me worthy again to be called your child. Amen.

Thursday

Lord Jesus Christ, in your life amongst us you spoke of your
Father, you blessed and healed, you called and forgave.
At the Last Supper you gave us the gift of your Body
and Blood. With your apostles you shared your ministry
and called others to follow you. May those who serve
you as our priests and ministers remain holy in their
union with you. Amen.

Friday

By the example of your love for us, Lord, you showed us
how to love others. By your creative power you gave
life to the world. In matrimony two people pledge to
each other their full and abiding love and are fruitful
in bringing forth new life. Bless them and guard them,
so that the example of your love may keep them one in
you. Amen.

Saturday

You have united us to you, Lord, by the waters of baptism.
You healed our souls and fed us with your Body and
Blood. In our times of sickness we ask your gift of
bodily anointing to cure us from our frailty, to grant
us your grace and to prepare us to meet you in eternity.
May your bountiful love heal body and soul and raise us
up to you. Amen.

"Above all, maintain constant love for one another....Be hospitable to one another without complaining...serve one another with whatever gift each of you has received."

1 Pet. 4: 8-10

SUNDAY

Dear Lord, be with the leaders of our church.

Give them holy wisdom, a store of courage, an open heart.

Be with them as they care for your church and its people.

May the Holy Spirit rest on them to confirm their faith,

to bless and guide them each and every day. Amen.

MONDAY

With you my God, my parents gave me life in this world.

I ask you, give them life with you in eternity. Amen.

TUESDAY

Lord, help me to remember that my parents/children are
   human, as I am.

Help me to appreciate that they are struggling with
   problems, as I am.

Help me to see that they are much hurt by neglect, as I am.

Help me to understand that they are moved by love, as I am.

Help me to realize that we are not so very different after all!
   Amen.

WEDNESDAY

So many, Lord, have gone before me – parents, grand-
   parents and those before them.

Make me grateful for my family and may they all have
   eternal rest with you. Amen.

THURSDAY

Bless the efforts of scientists who work to overcome illnesses in our world. Enlighten their minds, strengthen their resolve, inspire their initiatives. May their efforts relieve pain and suffering, and restore good health. I ask this through Christ our Lord. Amen.

FRIDAY

Lord, may our courts and our lawyers be observant of law, measured in justice, dedicated to equity. May they be fair, balanced and honest. Amen.

SATURDAY

May those who rule our country do so in the interests of all, in wisdom of legislation and in right governance. May they work for the common good, but preserve the rights and the dignity of each individual. May they learn from the past, safeguard the present and secure the future. May they have a sense of service and be upright in all their dealings. Amen.

*"I have loved you with an everlasting love; therefore
I have continued my faithfulness to you."*

JER. 31: 3

SUNDAY

Lord, I am pressed from every side.
My spirit fails as troubles grow.
Lift up my heart, make firm my will.
Shield me now from each new blow.

MONDAY

You, Lord, are my surest hope,
for you are God of truth and right.
I trust you, Lord, and plead with you
to bring me now from dark to light. Amen.

TUESDAY

Lord, I am having a hard day.
Bring me a smile. Amen.

WEDNESDAY

Lord, help me to be me, instead of trying to be someone else.
In creating me you made me special and you love me just
   as I am. Amen.

THURSDAY

Smiles freeze over, tears well up, heart skips a beat.
It seems like one of those days.
But God reigns, mercy flows, grace abounds.
And these lift me out of my daze. Amen.

FRIDAY

Dear God, I'm facing some rough times today.
Help me tough it out. Amen.

SATURDAY

Lord, I've stumbled along today.
Forgive me the mess, the thinking of me.
Remember the good I've striven to do,
And bring back my focus to you. Amen.

AUGUST

WEEK 32 A DAY WITH GOD

"...God chose you as the first fruits for salvation through sanctification by the Spirit and through belief in the truth."

2 Thess. 2: 13

Sunday

Dear God, you are light to my mind, light to my heart,
   light to my soul.
Keep shining in me, so that I may never be left in the dark.
   Amen.

Monday

Lord, I have many things to do today.
Keep me focused, calm and willing. Amen.

Tuesday

I can give without loving.
Save me from this, Lord.
But I cannot love without giving.
Help me to be generous in hand and heart. Amen.

Wednesday

Lord, I am lonely today.
Let's stay together for a while. Amen.

THURSDAY

Dear Lord, you love me now and for always.

Help me be worthy of that love now and for always.

Dear Lord, I love you now and for always.

Help me to be true to that love now and for always. Amen.

FRIDAY

Lord, so much is grabbing my attention today.

Help me not to lose sight of you in the jumble. Amen.

SATURDAY

Dear Lord, so often my life feels pretty humdrum.

Maybe I'm getting nowhere getting things done.

Did you ever feel the same when you were on earth? Amen.

WEEK 33 JOY IN THE LORD

"…your hearts will rejoice, and no one will take your joy from you."
JOHN 16: 22

SUNDAY

The joy of knowing you,
The joy of loving you,
The joy of praising you.
These are the greatest of joys.
May I treasure these always. Amen.

MONDAY

Lord, I offer you all that I am, all that I will be
For in you and for you I find my fulfilment. Amen.

TUESDAY

My deepest joy is found in my God,
With nothing else to compare it.
The joy I receive in loving my God,
Will be doubled and blessed when I share it. Amen.

WEDNESDAY

God's love forgives my sin,
God's love leads me back to him.
Lord, grant me these joys always. Amen.

THURSDAY

I rejoice in your presence, Lord.
I rejoice in your love.
I rejoice in your graces given,
And the glory that shines from above. Amen.

FRIDAY

Dear Lord, I've just had a wonderful time with my family/
friends. I could feel their love, their respect, their
support around me. I hope that I radiated the same to
them. Thank you, Lord, for the good time, the joyous
moments, for the love. May our happy memories sustain
us. I ask you to bless them all – and me too. Amen.

SATURDAY

Lord, I hold my faith and it holds me.

Help me to reach out and share it with others,

And let them be part of my joy. Amen.

WEEK 34 THE CHURCH

*"…set the believers an example in speech and
conduct, in love, in faith…"*

1 Tim. 4: 12

Sunday

When Christ ascended to heaven he left his disciples the
church to continue his work. The church today embraces
the world far and wide to continue the work of Christ.
Dear Lord, keep it on track. Amen.

Monday

O Lord, the apostles you chose were a motley crew – full of
fervour, doubts, pride, love, hard-headedness, devotion,
fear, self-centredness, timidity, trust, distractedness,
even treachery. But you chose them. You moulded
them and graced them for their task. As your apostle
today, I ask you Lord, for your same care, for your same
guidance, for your same grace. Amen.

Tuesday

It was on Peter that Christ built his church for the world.
Lord, help me be willing like Peter today. Amen.

WEDNESDAY

Your church, Lord, is called

– to be one – united with you;

– to be holy – living with your grace;

– to be catholic – reaching lovingly to all;

– to be apostolic – faithful to its inheritance.

May it be so in every way and every day.

And as I am church, may I too be so every day. Amen.

THURSDAY

It is through your church, Lord, that you give me so many
of your graces – grace of the sacraments, of blessings, of
community, of prayer. May the church always stand sure
in faith, courageous in action, wise in decision. Let it
always remember that it is your church. Amen.

FRIDAY

May I with the church praise God.

May I by the church affirm God's Word.

May I through the church work for the betterment of all.

May I in the church be a sign of communion among all its
members. Amen.

SATURDAY

Lord Jesus Christ, you offered all when you bled and
died on the Cross. But you gave me even more – the
Eucharist of your Body and Blood to be with me
every day. Through the ministry of the church, may I
accept it as your gift, receive it as your life, adore it as
your memory, and take it to myself as food for heaven.
Amen.

WEEK 35 JESUS WITH ME

"…it is no longer I who live, but it is Christ who lives in me. And the life I now live in the flesh I live by faith in the Son of God."

Gal. 2: 20

Sunday

Jesus, Son of God and Son of Mary, be with me as I come before you to honour, to praise, to adore you. May I see in you the wonders of the world and sense your presence with me each day. Amen.

Monday

The Messiah was long promised.
The Saviour was long desired.
The Lord was long awaited.
But when he came so many turned aside.
May I receive him as Messiah, thank him as Saviour,
and adore him as Lord. Amen.

Tuesday

O Jesus, present in the Holy Eucharist, may I praise you as really present,
and receive you with joy and expectation. Amen.

WEDNESDAY

May the Bread of Life be for me the font of life,
Now and for always. Amen.

THURSDAY

Jesus descended from the Father,
  but remained in the Trinity.
Jesus died on the Cross,
  but stayed living at Easter.
Jesus ascended to the Father,
  but remained in the Eucharist.
May I always praise him. Amen.

FRIDAY

Jesus taught, Jesus healed, Jesus saved
  for all the world – and for me. Amen.

Saturday

Jesus came to tell of the Kingdom, the Kingdom of justice
and peace, which must be in the hearts of all who follow
him. He speaks to us of his Kingdom still today. I ask
you, Lord, help me build that Kingdom first of all in my
own life, so that it may come to be in the lives of others.
Amen.

SEPTEMBER

WEEK 36 HELP ME, LORD

"...do not fear, for I am with you, do not be afraid, for I am your God; I will strengthen you,
I will help you, I will uphold you..."

Is. 41: 10

SUNDAY

To know lots of things is knowledge,
To deal rightly with them is wisdom.
Help me always to act like this,
To see you as the one from whom all wisdom comes,
And to whom all wisdom rightly leads. Amen.

MONDAY

Lord, I may have made a fool of myself today.
Help me pick myself up again. Amen.

TUESDAY

Truth brings freedom, truth makes right, truth upholds justice.
Help me to be a person of truth in my words, in my
thoughts and in my judgments. Amen.

WEDNESDAY

Save me, Lord, from the sin of pride.
A little self doubt can be a good thing. Amen.

Thursday

When I was born I was so small, so fragile, so dependent.
As I grew I become tall and strong and independent.
But I am still small in your eyes, Lord, liable to buckle and break,
And so dependent on your love and care.
Let me never forget this. Amen.

Friday

I have received much.
Help me to give much.
And all in your name. Amen.

Saturday

I need you Lord, when I start the day,
I need you Lord, when I hit the pace.
I need you Lord, when I strive to win.
I need you Lord, when I fall on my face.

I need you Lord, when I prance in pride.
I need you Lord, when I start to shout.
I need you Lord, to remind me too
I have much to be humble about. Amen.

WEEK 37 DEATH

"If we have died with him, we will also live with him;

if we endure, we will also reign with him…"

2 Tim. 2: 11, 12

Sunday

Dear Lord, death seems an end for so many, but it's only
the door to life with you and the joys of eternity. Help
me keep my death in its true perspective and prepare for
it with calmness and trust. Our meeting will be joyous.
Amen.

Monday

When I die I shall be more alive than ever,
for I shall be in the arms of the eternal God. Amen.

Tuesday

Death comes but once.
Christ often. Amen.

WEDNESDAY

Jesus died and arose to his Father.
Some day I shall die. May I rise to be with them. Amen.

THURSDAY

So much of my time, Lord, is spent in waiting.
At the check-out, at the bus, at the airport.
It seems such a waste of time.
But my life on earth is surely a time of waiting,
of waiting to come to completion in eternity.
It is God's time for me to grow with him,
to reach for his love, to be filled with his grace.
It is God's time for me.
Let me not waste it. Amen.

FRIDAY

Earth is but the door,
Heaven is the home.
Lead me safely there, Lord. Amen.

SATURDAY

I pray for all who may die today, facing death in great pain,
  in fear or alone.
Dear Lord, be with them urgently, and in your great mercy.
  Amen.

WEEK 38 MY FAMILY

"See what love the Father has given us, that we should be
called children of God; and that is what we are."

1 JOHN 3: 1

SUNDAY

For the gift of my parents, I thank you Lord.
For the gift of my brothers and sisters and friends,
    I thank you Lord.
For the gift of my wider family, I thank you Lord.
May I love them, honour them and always stand by them.
    Amen.

MONDAY

When we gather together as a family,
To eat, to play, to rest, to pray,
Be with us and protect us, Lord,
And bless us night and day. Amen.

TUESDAY

Children are the highest gift to parents in this world. May
    they see in them the imprint of God and lead them in
    the ways of right. Amen.

WEDNESDAY

O Lord, grant to all fathers of families the strength to be
provident, the tenderness to be loving and the will to
be faithful. May they be good examples to those who
depend on them. May they be blessed in the shelter
and happy home they provide, and may the grace of
God keep them resolute, temperate, gentle and devout.
Amen.

THURSDAY

To all mothers, Lord, you have given the surpassing role
to bear new life, to give birth to the generations of
tomorrow. May mothers respect this privilege, be
thankful for it and be constant in its demands. May they
bring joy, harmony, stability and graciousness to their
family. May you bless them and keep them close to you.
Amen.

Friday

Dear Lord, I pray today for all those families torn apart
by alcohol, domestic violence, sexual abuse, gambling
and drugs. May those who are responsible for these
come to acknowledge their faults and work to turn their
lives around. May those who are subjected to these be
comforted by your help, take courageous steps to avoid
the damage and suffering and to protect the innocent.
Amen.

Saturday

Like the family of the Trinity,
like the family of Nazareth,
Lord, help me make my family one of love and care. Amen.

WEEK 39 REACHING TO OTHERS

"The Lord is near to the broken-hearted, and
    saves the crushed in spirit."

Ps. 34: 18

SUNDAY

Lord, give me a kindly mind, kindly words and a kindly heart.
May I think well of others, speak well of them and hold
    them with gentleness. Amen.

MONDAY

Sometimes through malice, sometimes through jealousy,
    sometimes in error,
the good reputation of people is impugned, or scarred, or
    destroyed.
Dear Lord, grant that this terrible injustice be quickly
    rectified,
that those at fault repair the damage done by their words or
    actions,
and that the ones hurt may be restored to good grace. Amen.

TUESDAY

Friends console, uplift and complete me.
May I also do likewise for them. Amen.

Wednesday

If love is to be shared, as it ought to be,
Then Lord, I'm sure it's up to me. Amen.

Thursday

Oh Lord, I've been involved in an awful row!
I lost my temper, boiled over, blew my top.
Help me to become calm again and cool.
Help me to apologize for lashing out,
And for whatever hurt I may have caused to others. Amen.

Friday

Jesus, you humbled yourself to serve us in this world.
May I be not proud to serve those in need.
Jesus, you humbled yourself to serve us in this world.
May I be like you and follow your lead. Amen.

SATURDAY

When others call for help, Lord, may I come to them as you
came,

in compassion, concern and love and solely for their good,
not mine. Amen.

OCTOBER

WEEK 40 GLORY TO GOD

"…that God may be glorified in all things through Jesus Christ. To him belong the glory and the power for ever and ever. Amen."

1 Pet. 4: 11

Sunday

I pray for lots of things – for health, for wealth, for
  happiness.
But what I should pray for most of all is that God be ever
  glorified.
Lord, help me to be less selfish in my prayer. Amen.

Monday

I give glory to you God, for all the wonders you have done.
I give glory to you God, for all the love that you have shown.
But I give glory to you God, most of all, because you are
  God. Amen.

Tuesday

May my words glorify you, Lord.
May my actions glorify you, Lord.
May even my silences glorify you, Lord. Amen.

WEDNESDAY

The wonders of modern technology,
Are terrific and marvellous and new.
But the best thing of all for me each day,
Is to link up and talk, Lord, with you. Amen.

THURSDAY

May God be praised in the glory of the skies,
    in the deeps of the ocean, in the wonders of the earth.
But above all else, may God be glorified
    in the minds and hearts of men and women. Amen.

FRIDAY

Glory to God in all of creation.
    Glory, glory, glory.
Glory to God for the gift of salvation.
    Glory, glory, glory. Amen.

SATURDAY

Let me remember your greatness O God,
And the love in which you made me.
Let me remember your mercy O God,
And the love by which you forgave me. Amen.

WEEK 41 LORD, BE WITH ME

"The Lord is my light and my salvation; whom shall I fear? The Lord is the stronghold of my life; of whom shall I be afraid?"

Ps. 27: 1

SUNDAY

Lord, yesterday gave birth to today, and today will spring
  into tomorrow.
Help me to remember that what I was, what I am and what
  I shall be is just another part of my living.
May you be with me each day. Amen.

MONDAY

Lord, I am on a journey, a journey in this world,
  a journey to another.
There are bright days and sad days, graces, failures, prayers
  and friends, smiles and tears and ups and downs.
But through it all I sense a presence, the presence of you my
  loving God.
Be with me always and draw me to you. Amen.

TUESDAY

Lord, I am hurting in my heart today.
Give me strength to deal with anguish. Amen.

WEDNESDAY

You listen to me always when I call, Lord.
May I always be attentive to you when you answer. Amen.

THURSDAY

Dear God, I feel lonely today, overlooked, forgotten, sad.
Help me sense your presence Lord. Stand by me now and
    for ever. Amen.

FRIDAY

Lord, have mercy
    on those who have fallen today.
Christ have mercy
    on those who forget you today.
Lord have mercy
    on me as I journey today. Amen.

SATURDAY

Lord, I know that you are with me, even when I do not see you.
Lord, I know that you are with me, even when I do not hear you.
Lord, I know that you are with me, even when I do not sense you.
Lord, help me see you, hear you, feel you. Amen.

WEEK 42 FOR PEACE (II)

"Peace I leave with you; my peace I give to you. I do not give to you as the world gives. Do not let your hearts be troubled…"

John 14: 27

SUNDAY

Lord Jesus, you reminded us that you and the Father are one, that you came to do his will, and that in seeing you we would see your Father. Your unity with him, in the unity of the Blessed Trinity, gave us the perfect example of being one with each other. Grant us the will, the strength and the determination also to be one with each other and to rejoice in our unity of heart and mind. Amen.

MONDAY

Our human history has been marred by so many wars among nations – so many have died, so many have suffered, so many have been displaced. We ask you, Lord, to grant us the maturity to look to justice, to equity, to mercy, to pity, so that we avoid the conflicts and come to peace. Amen.

TUESDAY

Dear Lord, our world is blessed by the richness of a great diversity of race, colour and culture. In these the people take a natural pride. They enrich their lives and the lives of others. As we treasure that which makes us to be what we are, so may we respect that which makes others to be what they are. Amen.

WEDNESDAY

God our Father, among the peoples of this earth we see a range of religious beliefs and practices. May what is good in each of these lead not to conflict, but to mutual acceptance and respect. Amen.

THURSDAY

Lord Jesus Christ, you came among us to establish God's kingdom, and called us to be one as you are with the Father. Throughout our history we have not been heedful of that call. Help us look to those things that we hold in common as the source of strength to deal with what divides us. Grant us humility, courage and goodwill to work towards full Christian unity in you. Amen.

Friday

Dear Lord, it is in the heart of our family that we are born, loved and raised. It is the basis of our identity and the seed-bed of our future. But sometimes the precious bond of family peace and accord is torn apart. Help us rise above apportioning blame and move with sincerity to restore the harmony and joy which should be alive in our family. Amen.

Saturday

In many ways, Lord, people are different by race, religion, sex, colour, political persuasion, culture, language. Give us a heart and a mind big enough to recognize that we are all, in one way or another, different – not in ourselves better or worse – just different. May we acknowledge honestly, accept genuinely and respect fully those who are different from ourselves. May our accepted diversity be the foundation of our unity. Amen.

WEEK 43 SPECIAL GROUPS (II)

"How does God's love abide in anyone who...sees a
brother or sister in need and yet refuses help?"

1 JOHN 3: 17

SUNDAY

Dear Lord, I hold my child tenderly and lovingly in my heart.
The miracle of his/her birth was a reflection of your creative power.
The warmth of his/her closeness is a shadow of your presence.
The smile on his/her face is a sign of your embracing love.
The grasp of his/her hands is an assurance of your support.
So much of you, dear Lord, shines out from this child.
By loving him/her may I grow to love you even more.
    Amen.

MONDAY

In a wonderful way, Lord, you have gifted men and
    women to be artists, writers, musicians, performers.
    May they be enriched in their gifts, and use them to
    touch our souls, to uplift our hearts, to bring us joy.
    May they be thankful for their talents and realize
    their responsibilities in using them – responsibilities
    to themselves, to their audiences, and to truth and
    goodness. Amen.

TUESDAY

Those who teach our children have a unique role in helping them develop, and in preparing the men and women of the world of tomorrow. May all teachers gain a deep realization of their special privilege. Give them wisdom, patience, resilience, responsibility and a sense of wonder for their students. May they be true collaborators with the parents of their pupils. May God bless them in their task. Amen.

WEDNESDAY

In various parts of the world men and women are being persecuted for their religious beliefs, sometimes in violent ways, sometimes in ways less open, yet just as vicious. I pray you Lord, confirm them in their beliefs, give them the physical and moral strength to stand firm, comfort them in their sufferings. May their devout constancy bring about a softening of the hearts and an enlightening of the minds of those persecuting them. May the steadfastness of those suffering be a lesson for us and a grace to make strong within us our own faith and will. Amen.

Thursday

O Lord, I pray today for all the deceased military men and women of our nation. So many gave their lives, perhaps in fear and trembling, so many bore their wounds, certainly in pain and suffering. I ask you, Lord, to reward their sacrifices and grant consolation to their families and friends. Amen.

Friday

I grieve for those lives lost and for injuries sustained in road accidents. May all drivers understand and take their responsibility of care seriously as they drive on our roads. May they be patient, alert, sober, and may they be considerate of others. Amen.

SATURDAY

Dear Lord, I pray for all who lie in our local cemetery. They lived their lives as fathers, mothers, husbands, wives, sons and daughters. Each had a span of years, some short, some long, before they passed to eternal life with you. They were blessed in their years with love and joy, but at times found burdens and sorrows hard to bear. But now dear Lord, their earthly life is over, and they rest at last in your hands. Reward the good they have done, their perseverance and their struggle, as you are a God of love. Forgive whatever wrong they committed through human frailty, for you are also a God of mercy. In your gracious favour treat them lovingly and mercifully, for their eternal happiness and for your everlasting glory. Amen.

WEEK 44 THE WAYS OF LIFE

"His divine power has given us everything
needed for life and godliness…"

2 PET. 1: 3

SUNDAY

Jesus told us to set no bounds to our love, as his heavenly
Father set none to his. At times I make my love
conditional, or hem it in with demands on others. May
my love be not selfish. Dear Lord, help me to give my
love to others in the measure that you have given yours
to me. Amen.

MONDAY

Dear Lord, I pray that I may see your good in others.
I pray also that they may see your good in me. Amen.

TUESDAY

Liking is not loving, lust is not love.
O dear Lord, give me the sense to know the difference,
the wisdom to appreciate the value of each,
and the courage to stand firm
    when I am tempted to mix them up. Amen.

WEDNESDAY

Lord, I'm not sure what the rest of the day will bring.
Whatever it may be, I ask you to save me from harm
and keep me close to you. Amen.

THURSDAY

Christ Jesus, our Lord, you spoke the words of salvation,
truth and promise.
Help me to listen to you always and make your words the
guidelines of my life. Amen.

FRIDAY

Dear Lord, forgive me when I have sinned.
But especially, Lord, forgive me when I forget that I have.
Amen.

SATURDAY

Lord, it has been a long hard day.
Give me a quiet night and a rested awakening. Amen.

NOVEMBER

WEEK 45 I PRAY FOR OTHERS (II)

"Let the word of Christ dwell in you richly; teach and admonish one another in all wisdom."

COL. 3: 16

SUNDAY

O Lord, may I be loving as you are,
caring as you are, gentle as you are.
May I reach out to those in need,
and may I never count the cost. Amen.

MONDAY

My faith is in you, Lord.
It gives me eyes to see you, ears to hear you, a heart to love you.
May I see and hear and love you in others all around me.
Amen.

TUESDAY

Lord, may my heart grow more loving,
My hands more open, my spirit more willing,
My praise more constant, my forgiving more prompt,
My faith more firm, my caring more selfless,
My hope more sure, my giving more generous. Amen.

WEDNESDAY

In others I see good, in others I see bad.

In others I see joy, in others I see sorrow.

They see the same in me,

for we are all brothers and sisters.

Unite us in joy. Amen.

THURSDAY

I depend on you.

Others depend on me.

Enable me, Lord. Amen.

FRIDAY

Lord, I am loved by so many people.

Make me conscious of their love, worthy of their love.

Make me accepting of their love, respectful of their love.

Help me to repay their love in all the ways I can,

for in loving me they show me just a little glimpse of you.

Amen.

SATURDAY

Lord, give me a warm heart,

a willing ear, an open hand.

So that I may share your gifts with others. Amen.

WEEK 46 THANKS BE TO GOD (III)

"Worship the Lord with gladness;...Enter his gates
with thanksgiving, and his courts with praise.
Give thanks to him, bless his name."

Ps. 100: 2, 4

SUNDAY

Lord, I thank you for the little things on earth, for the great
and mighty things,
for the things that fascinate and amaze me, for the things I
have and use.
I give thanks, Lord, for all creation, but most of all for you,
the Creator. Amen.

MONDAY

I stand in thankfulness before you, Lord, for all that you
have given me, shown me, promised me, and for your
protection and guidance. Amen.

TUESDAY

Lord, I thank you for the food you give me to eat. Bless
those who grow it and prepare it.

As it gives me strength I ask you to grant sustenance to
those who lack it. Amen.

WEDNESDAY

God our Father, in your greatest act of love you sent your
Son, Jesus Christ, to be one with us in this world. By his
teaching and his sacrifice we are enabled to be one with
you in eternity. May our thanks be a reflection of the
immensity of your love. Amen.

THURSDAY

Thank you, Lord, for fleas and snakes and things that bite.
They help us appreciate the ones that don't. Amen.

FRIDAY

Thanks for mother's care, father's fidelity, friend's
companionship, the help of generous people, but most
of all I thank you Lord, for your constant love. Amen.

SATURDAY

Lord, I always seem to be asking you for something – for me, for friends, for others. Forgive me if at times I do not return thanks to you for your answers to my prayers. It's not deliberate that I do not do it, it's just that life gets pretty busy much of the time. But now Lord, in calm and quiet, with earnestness and gratitude, I offer thanks for all your gifts, for all your blessings, for the abundance of your graces. I thank you for your constant care, your overflowing kindnesses, your open-handed goodness. May I be always grateful to you, the greatest of all givers. And forgive me in advance, for the next time I forget to say thanks. Amen.

WEEK 47 SPECIAL GROUPS (III)

*"By this everyone will know that you are my
disciples, if you have love for one another."*

JOHN 13: 35

SUNDAY

I ask you Lord, to look with special kindness on the young
of our country, as they grow into adult maturity and
seek to set the pattern of their future lives. Guide
them in their decisions, inspire them in their planning,
protect them in their judgments. Be with them as they
make the choices which determine their coming years.
Amen.

MONDAY

Over the passage of the years we move into our old age.
With it comes rest and calm and a quiet and special
wisdom. We ask you Lord, to bless all people in their
later years, assure them of sufficient physical care,
bring comfort to those alone, relief to those suffering
and grant them the warmth of the love of family and
friends. Amen.

TUESDAY

Dear Lord, at this moment so many people are on the roads, in the air, or on the sea travelling from place to place. Whatever their reason they are on the move. Grant them safe passage, pleasant travelling, and a sure return to their families and friends. Amen.

WEDNESDAY

Lord, I ask you to take special care of new immigrants to our land. They have come here for a better way of life for themselves and their families. Help them as they make major changes in their lives, relieve the burdens of settling in to new customs, language and work. Inspire our people to be welcoming and of help. Amen.

THURSDAY

I ask you Lord, to have a special regard for those people who are refugees from their own homes. As you had to flee to another land for safety's sake, many of these have had to do likewise. Give them your protection and the help of kindly people. Relieve their plight and grant them a safe return to their homelands. Amen.

FRIDAY

I pray Lord, for those who have just lost family or friends through death. May they be consoled in knowing that you have called their loved ones home to you and may they be comforted in recalling the good memories of their times together. Amen.

SATURDAY

For those in prison, Lord, I pray. Whatever wrong they have done, be merciful to them. Whatever harm they have occasioned, grant healing. Bring them to a reformed state of mind and a firm resolve to change their lives. Amen.

WEEK 48 ADVENT

"…the Lord waits to be gracious to you; therefore he will rise up to show mercy to you…blessed are all those who wait for him."
Is. 30: 18

SUNDAY

God created the world and set it in motion.
God spoke to men and women and made a covenant with
them.
But when they proved that they would not listen,
God sent them a Messiah, a Saviour, Lord,
a little babe born poor in a stable cold.
And then the whole world took on a new creation.
Oh God, may we never cease to thank you for that child.
Amen.

MONDAY

I stand and wait for the Christ who comes
For he will be born on Christmas day.
May I be there to welcome him,
And never say him nay. Amen.

TUESDAY

May the coming of Christ to awaken the world sound a call
in me that will ring all the days of my life, "The Saviour
is here!" Help me to be with him each day. Amen.

WEDNESDAY

Mary waited in quiet hope
'Til the day her Son was born.
May I in gladness wait for him,
And greet that glorious morn. Amen.

THURSDAY

My Christ is coming,
Wait in gathering joy.
My Christ is coming,
Welcome the little boy. Amen.

FRIDAY

Lord, may I prepare my heart to welcome the birth of your Son.
May his birth come to fullness in me. Amen.

SATURDAY

Three wise men bowed before him when he came.

May I bow down in homage at his birth,

For he is my Saviour, my Lord and King,

His coming gave restoring hope to earth. Amen.

DECEMBER

WEEK 49 SECURE IN GOD

*"…I will come again and will take you to myself, so
that where I am, there you may be also."*

JOHN 14: 3

SUNDAY

'Midst the worries of my world I look to you, Lord – safe in
the reality of your care for me, sure of the truth of your
promises to me, and happy in the knowledge of your
presence with me. Amen.

MONDAY

Father creator, Son redeemer, Spirit consoler,
I rest in you – secure, saved, blessed. Amen.

TUESDAY

The power of God guides me on my path through life. May
I be always thankful for his mighty help. Amen.

WEDNESDAY

Dear Lord, if ever I feel alone may I reach to you,
Secure in heart and mind and in my spirit
that you are always close by me in loving presence. Amen.

THURSDAY

The peace of God surrounds me. The love of God embraces me.
The hand of God directs me. The grace of God sustains me.
The gifts of God enrich me. The presence of God uplifts me.
O Lord, I am blessed beyond all telling. Amen.

FRIDAY

"With him, through him, in him."
These are the guideposts of my journey.
I thank you Lord, and travel secure with you. Amen.

SATURDAY

Jesus, our Saviour, you died for us when we were still
sinners and your death saved us from the retribution
of God. Through you we gained our reconciliation and
are filled with joyful trust in God. I rest secure, for in
the certainty of your saving promises you give me hope
upon hope. For this I thank you from the depths of my
heart. Amen.

WEEK 50 TO BE LIKE CHRIST

"...you have been raised with Christ, seek the things that are above, where Christ, is seated at the right hand of God...then...you will be revealed with him in glory."

Col. 3: 1, 4

SUNDAY

Christ came into our world to teach us the truth.
Christ came into our world to heal us from sin.
Christ came into our world to show us the way.
May I hold the truth, fall not into sin, and walk his way.
Amen.

MONDAY

May I become more like Christ in his mercy, in his giving, in his sacrifice, in his love. Amen.

TUESDAY

Christ's coming was our becoming – becoming blessed, becoming graced, becoming redeemed.
Help me, Lord, remember this. Amen.

WEDNESDAY

Christ's life was lived for others.
May I live likewise for others and for God. Amen.

THURSDAY

Christ came meek and mild – yet he condemned the
hypocrites and liars.

Christ came kind and gentle – yet he whipped the traders
out of the temple.

May I be meek and mild, and kind and gentle – but full of
passion for your name. Amen.

FRIDAY

Christ came not in glory, but in a lowly stable,
His life was cloaked in humility.
He lowered himself to become the servant of all.
He died like a criminal upon the Cross.
Lord, when I get too puffed up about myself,
help me to be like Christ in his humbleness.
For in that was the source of his glory. Amen.

SATURDAY

To walk in the footsteps of Christ is to walk in giving and
caring, in blessing and helping, in suffering and pain, in
sorrow and anguish, in wonder and glory.

May I walk that path resolutely in his shadow and come to
eternal life with him. Amen.

WEEK 51 CHRISTMAS

"…the Word became flesh and lived among us, and
we have seen his glory, the glory of a father's
only son, full of grace and truth."

JOHN 1: 14

SUNDAY

Hail blessed Christmas Day, O God,
Your Son was born that day.
Born to save a fallen world,
Born to banish sin away.

MONDAY

Born to Mary, chosen one,
Born to form our world anew,
Born to raise us up again,
Born to draw us all to you.

TUESDAY

Born to bring his hope to us,
Born to be the saving One.
May we praise you, God on high,
And welcome now your Saviour Son. Amen.

WEDNESDAY

A whole world was wrapped up in the Christmas Child.

As it unfolded, the grace and the mercy of God was
showered on humankind.

May this Child be a light to me and may I reach out to
receive the gift of his presence. Amen.

THURSDAY

A virgin will bear a Son, the scriptures told us, and the wait
was hard and long.

But then he came and told Good News, but many stopped
their ears.

May I open wide my mind and heart to heed his words and
walk with him. Amen.

FRIDAY

The Christ has come, the angels sang,
The anointed one is here.
May he find room in my poor heart,
To bring me joy, to banish fear. Amen.

SATURDAY

Before that tiny babe – a maiden mother, a guardian father,
a choir of angels, bedazzled shepherds, adoring kings.

All stood and gazed and pondered and drew breath,
for in that moment the world was still in silent wonder.
Amen.

WEEK 52 END OF THE YEAR

"...remember, I am with you always, to the end of the age."
MATT. 28: 20

SUNDAY

So many good things happened for me in this past year – good
things I appreciated, good things I perhaps overlooked.
Thank you, Lord, for being there with me. Amen.

MONDAY

During this past year many friends have helped me in so
many ways, by their love, their acceptance and their
patience. I ask you Lord, to thank them for me by
showering on them your best blessings. Amen.

TUESDAY

Lord, you gave me the past year.
I offer it back with thanks.
Count it for my good, Lord. Amen.

WEDNESDAY

Lord, I could have learnt much during this past year – of
love, of friendship, of acceptance, of repentance, of
giving. I could have praised you more, drawn closer to
you, glorified your name. Sorry, Lord. Be with me as
this year draws to a close. Amen.